NATIONAL GEOGRAPHIC

Chocolate

Bronwyn Tainui

T0308251

Contents

Do you like chocolate?
Chocolate is sweet and delicious.
Let's see how chocolate is made!

Cocoa Beans

Chocolate is made from cocoa beans.
Cocoa beans are found in cocoa pods.
Cocoa pods grow on cocoa trees.
These trees grow in warm, wet places.

5

People cut cocoa pods off the tree. Then the pods are cut open. Cocoa beans are scooped out of the pods.

The cocoa beans are covered and put in a warm place.
The warmth brings out the flavor.
This makes the cocoa taste better.
Then the cocoa beans are dried.
The dried cocoa beans are sent to a factory.

At the Chocolate Factory

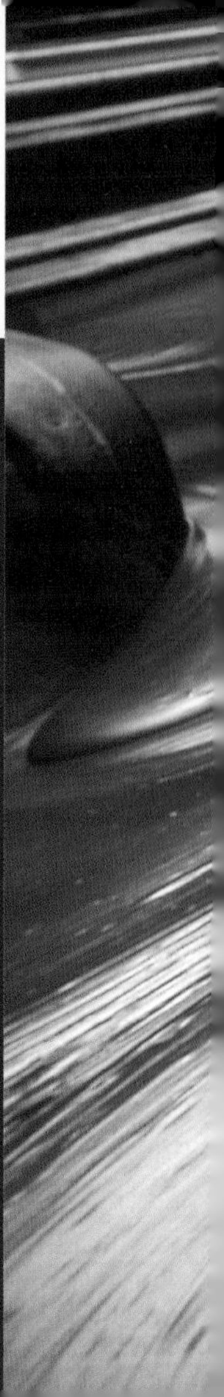

The cocoa beans are roasted in an oven. Then a machine removes the shells, or outer skins, of the cocoa beans. The cocoa beans are ground down. Milk and sugar are added to make a smooth chocolate liquid.

The chocolate is poured into molds
and made into different shapes.
Then the chocolate is left to cool.
As the chocolate cools, it becomes hard.
Finally, a machine wraps the chocolate.

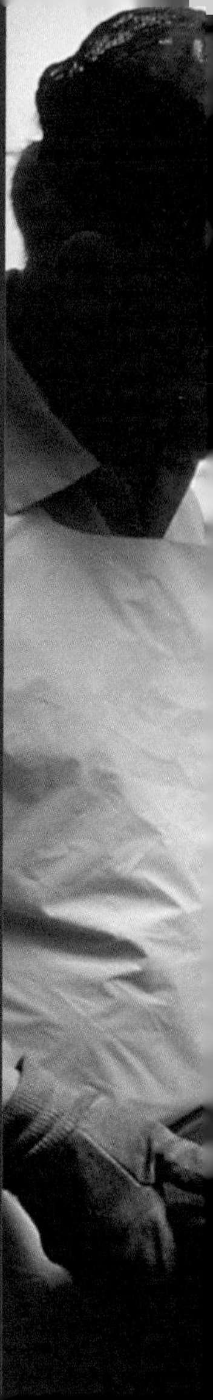

WILBUR
COATING

In the Store

The chocolate is packed into boxes.
Then it is sent to stores.
Now you can buy the chocolate.
How does it taste?

Glossary

cocoa beans — the seeds of a cocoa tree; they are used to make chocolate

cocoa pods — the fruit that grows on cocoa trees; they are full of cocoa beans

flavor — the taste of something

mold — a container used to shape food

roasted — cooked